A KID'S {GUIDE} to the NIGHT SKY

JOHN A. READ

CONSTELLATIONS ILLUSTRATED BY
FORD RASMUSSEN

sourcebooks
eXplore

Published by Sourcebooks eXplore, an imprint of Sourcebooks Kids.

P.O. Box 4410, Naperville, Illinois 60567-4410
(630) 961-3900
sourcebookskids.com

Originally published as *Learn to Stargaze* in 2022 in the United States of
America and Canada by Stellar Publishing.

Cataloging-in-Publication Data is on file with the Library of Congress.

Source of Production: Wing King Tong Paper Products Co. Ltd.,
Shenzhen, Guangdong Province, China
Date of Production: April 2024
Run Number: 5038802

Printed and bound in China.
WKT 10 9 8 7 6 5 4 3 2 1

To the parents, teachers, and other caring adults:

The careers of many astronauts, astronomers, and astrophysicists started with a night under the stars when a parent or teacher pointed at the sky and told a tale about what was there. Thanks for making stargazing a part of your kids' lives.

Contents

Chapter 1
Becoming a Stargazer

Have you ever wondered if there is life on other planets? Have you ever wondered where we came from? Have you ever wondered what our ancestors saw when they looked up at the sky? It is almost impossible not to ask these questions when you look up at the stars. The answers are out there, but some have yet to be discovered!

Stargazing fills us with wonder. It gives us hope for the future and reminds us of our past. We stargaze to connect with nature as well as our family and friends. We stargaze because it's fun!

Photons

A **photon** is a teeny tiny bit of light. When a photon hits the back of the eye, the brain assigns it a color!

When we stargaze, our eyes receive photons from the stars and planets. Those photons have traveled millions of kilometers from those planets and trillions of kilometers from the stars.

Do I Need a Telescope?

Almost everything mentioned in this book can be seen without a telescope. In many cases, you may need to get out of the city to view things like the Milky Way or a meteor shower.

What Is Stargazing?

Before the invention of the telescope in 1608, humans didn't know what stars and planets actually were. They simply looked at the sky with their eyes and tried to find meaning in what they saw. Stargazing is all about viewing the night sky with your eyes, just as people have done for thousands of years. Binoculars and telescopes enhance your ability to see faraway objects, but they are not necessary for stargazing.

What Is Space?

Space is everything outside Earth's atmosphere. Most countries agree that "space" is anything above one hundred kilometers (about sixty miles).

Archaeoastronomy

Ancient cultures built structures to track the movement of the stars and planets. These include Stonehenge in England and this Mayan pyramid at Chichén Itzá in Mexico.

The Stargazing Tool Kit

The most important thing while stargazing is to adapt your eyes to the dark. This means putting away light sources other than a red flashlight.

Instead of using phone apps, it's much better to use a guidebook (like this one) to chart your way across the sky.

It's also important to keep comfortable. Wear warm clothes, even in the summer, and have bug spray in the summer and fall.

Optional Accessories

Binoculars are recommended to magnify the deep-sky objects mentioned in this book. However, from dark skies, most of these objects can be seen with just your eyes. Note that some may only appear as tiny smudges of light.

The Moon and planets do not require dark skies. These objects look just as good from a city or town. Even the five brightest planets can be seen without a telescope. You will need a telescope to see Saturn's rings and Jupiter's moons.

Can I Take a Picture?

When attempting to photograph stars and planets, you are no longer stargazing; you are doing **astrophotography**. Astrophotography is far more challenging than stargazing. Taking photos of space typically requires special gear in addition to a camera.

Color

Cameras can see color in galaxies and nebulas, but our eyes cannot. Even with a telescope, galaxies and nebulas appear gray to the human eye.

Pro Tips

Dress Warm and Bring Liquid
Even during summer or in warm climates, it can get chilly at night. Be sure to dress for the cold! You may want to bring hot chocolate as well.

Bring a Chair
Stargazing from a chair, even if you're using binoculars or a telescope, makes the experience far more enjoyable.

Use a Red Light
Red headlamps make reading guidebooks (like this one) easy to do while maintaining your night vision.

Write It Down
A pencil is a very important stargazing tool. If you record your observations, your local astronomy club may send you a certificate for your observations.

What Are Stars?

Stars are giant balls of hot gas. Most stars are millions of times larger than Earth. When we look at the night sky, most of the stars we see are giant stars, far larger than our star, the Sun. This isn't because there are more of them. It is because giant stars are much brighter.

Stars come in all sorts of colors, sizes, and temperatures. Astronomers can tell a star's temperature from its color. Hot stars are blue, and cooler stars are red (but they are still hot). Some stars are always changing in size and brightness. These are called **variable stars**.

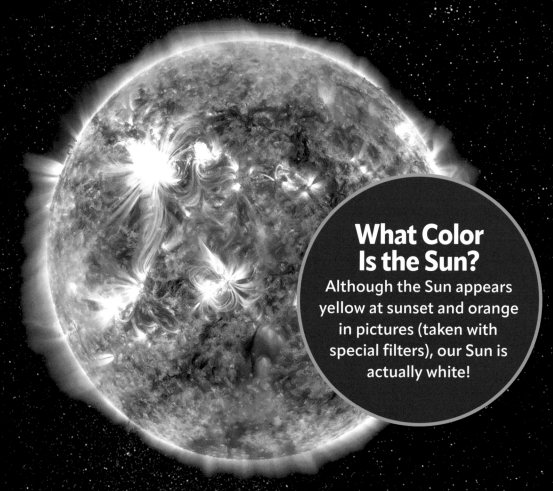

What Color Is the Sun?

Although the Sun appears yellow at sunset and orange in pictures (taken with special filters), our Sun is actually white!

The Life of a Star

Stars are born in great clouds of gas and dust. One gas cloud will form many stars of different sizes.

Regular Stars
Stars like our Sun live for billions of years.

Giant Stars
Larger stars burn through their fuel quickly and only live for a few million years.

Red Giants
When regular stars run low on fuel, they puff up into red giants.

Red Supergiants
These are some of the largest stars in the universe, but they are very short-lived.

Supernovas
Red supergiants explode so violently that they briefly shine as bright as billions of stars. The remaining mass becomes either a **neutron star** or a **black hole**.

Planetary Nebulas
Red giant stars eventually blow off their outer layers, which become nebulas.

White Dwarfs
A small ball of hot gas is all that is left of the original star.

Neutron Stars

Black Holes

What Are Planets?

Planets come in all different sizes and colors. Some of these worlds are rocky, and some are made only of gas. Some planets, like Earth, are mostly covered in water, while others are desert worlds, like Mars.

While stargazing, planets like Venus and Jupiter can be confused with bright stars. They often appear first shortly after sunset, before the stars.

Note: We will tour all the planets in our solar system in Chapter 5.

UFO? Nope, Just Venus

Venus is the cause of most UFO sightings. The planet is very bright, and when it is behind a tree or light clouds, it can appear to follow you wherever you go!

What Are Exoplanets?

Our solar system has eight planets and six dwarf planets (like Pluto). It's likely that almost every star has planets! Astronomers have found thousands of planets around other stars. Those planets are called exoplanets, which is short for extrasolar planets.

What Makes a Planet a Planet?

1. Planets **orbit** stars.
2. Planets are spherical.
3. Planets have cleaned their orbits of similarly sized objects.

Planet or Star?

If you're stargazing, how do you tell the difference between a planet and a star?

- The planets tend to be brighter than most stars.

- Planets are found near the **ecliptic**, the path the Sun takes across the sky.

- Planets change position from night to night. Jupiter and Saturn move slowly, so it may take you several weeks to notice.

- Use a free app such as Stellarium to determine the current position of each planet.

Jupiter as seen with the unaided eye

Jupiter as seen with binoculars

Jupiter as seen through a telescope

Jupiter as seen from a spacecraft

What Is the Milky Way Galaxy?

We live in a galaxy that contains over three hundred million stars. Its name is the Milky Way. If you look at the sky on a moonless night, far from city lights, you'll see it as a patchy star cloud that stretches across the sky.

The Milky Way also contains dark patches, known as dark nebulas. This is where dust obscures the stars.

What Is the Universe?

The universe includes all the stars, planets, galaxies, gas, dust, black holes, and, well, everything!

What Are Galaxies?

Galaxies are groups of billions and billions of stars. The most popular galaxy to observe (other than our own) is the Andromeda Galaxy (page 60). It can be observed without a telescope from dark skies. It is over two million **light-years** away!

Sky Glow

If you live in a city or town, your night sky is surprisingly bright. The sky is so bright that only the brightest stars are visible. But what makes the sky over a city so bright?

Sky glow, or light pollution, occurs when light from homes and businesses reaches the sky and is reflected back by the atmosphere. Sky glow hides most of the stars and the Milky Way.

The Moon also causes the sky to glow. If you are trying to see the Milky Way, it is best to attempt to see this during the new moon. See page 94–95 to learn more.

No clouds, but also no stars! Why is this?

Light also reflects off the ground, causing the sky to glow, especially during sports games!

Sky Glow Maps

Sky glow maps are a great way to find the best spots for stargazing. White, red, and yellow are towns and cities with lots of light pollution. Green (good), blue (better), and gray (best) are locations with dark skies.

of Fundy

NOVA SCOTIA

Halifax

www.lightpollutionmap.info

North Star

North Celestial Pole

Chapter 2
Movement of the Sky

Rising and Setting

Have you ever watched a sunrise or a sunset? You've probably noticed that the Sun rises in about the same place every day, and it sets on the opposite side of the sky. But why? Because Earth is spinning!

The Sun is not the only thing that rises and sets. The Moon and planets rise and set too. While standing on Earth, the sky appears to rotate around the **celestial poles** about once per day.

What Constellations Can You See?

Where you live determines what stars you can see. Unless you live on the equator, there are constellations you will never see! These stars are *always* blocked by Earth.

Look at this diagram, and imagine Earth spinning around its axis. If you were to live at the North Pole, you would only ever see half the sky!

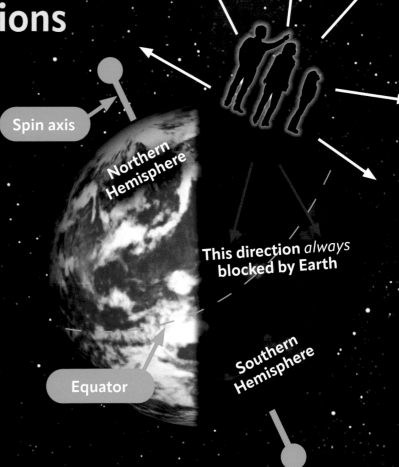

Spin axis

Northern Hemisphere

This direction *always* blocked by Earth

Southern Hemisphere

Equator

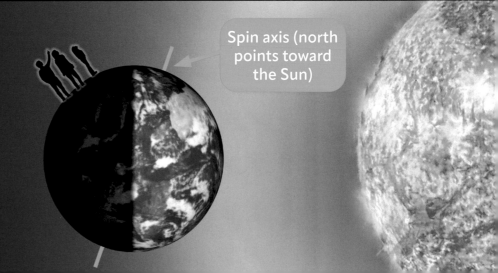

Summer Night Sky

Notice how close the stargazers are to the daytime side of Earth. This is why the nights are short and why the Sun is so much higher in the sky.

*Northern Hemisphere Seasons

Spin axis (north points toward the Sun)

Seasonal Skies

As Earth orbits the Sun over the course of the year, our view of the stars and constellations changes. This is why the maps in the next chapter are organized into seasons.

North Star

A long-exposure photograph pointed at the North Star will show the sky's rotation.

Why We Have Seasons

Earth's **spin axis** is tilted. This is why we have seasons. For half the year, where you live is tilted toward the Sun (spring and summer). For the other half of the year, you are tilted away from the Sun (fall and winter).

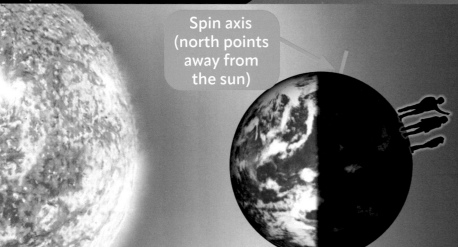

Spin axis (north points away from the sun)

Winter Night Sky

When tilted away from the Sun, notice how the same stargazers are closer to the plane of the solar system. This is why the Moon and planets appear higher in winter.

Finding North

As Earth turns on its axis, the entire sky appears to rotate, all except one star. Can you guess which one? Earth's spin axis points very close to the North Star, so the North Star hardly moves.

North Star's height (in degrees) above your horizon is always identical to your **latitude**. The further north you are, the higher this star will be.

Big Dipper (asterism)

North Star (Polaris)

Pointer stars (Merak and Dubhe)

Direction of sky rotation

Finding South

If you live south of the equator, you cannot see the North Star. And there is no bright star near the South Celestial Pole. To find south, you'll need to use the constellations on page 64 as a guide.

The North Star (aka Polaris) is not the brightest star in the sky. In fact, there are dozens of stars brighter than the North Star in the sky at any given time.

This way is north.

There is a region of the sky where the stars never dip below the **horizon**. This is called the **circumpolar** region. In this part of the sky, the stars appear to rotate around the North Star. Here is how the Big Dipper would appear in the evening sky during each season.

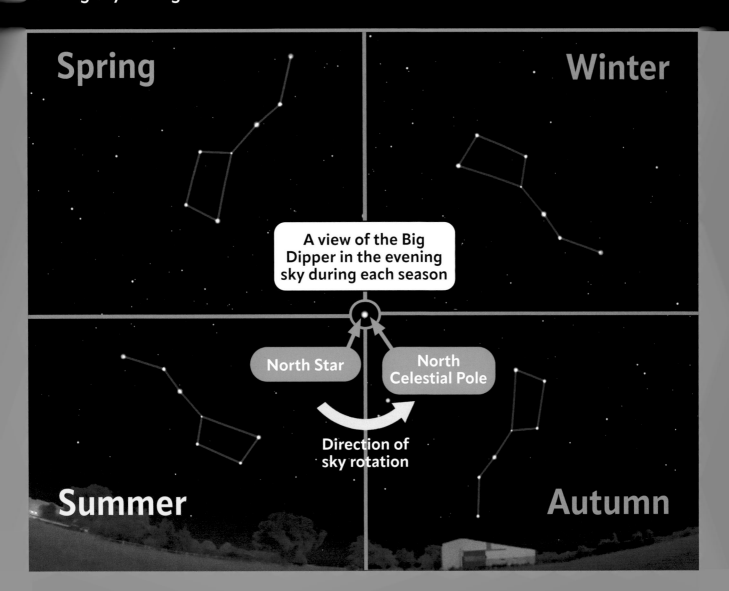

Spring

Winter

A view of the Big Dipper in the evening sky during each season

North Star

North Celestial Pole

Direction of sky rotation

Summer

Autumn

Chapter 3

Learn the Constellations

Official Constellations

The International Astronomical Union, or IAU, has divided the sky into eighty-eight different regions called constellations.

These "official" constellations are primarily used to name the stars and to tell other astronomers which part of the sky they are studying.

The Six Skies

As we learned in the previous chapter, the constellations visible in the evening sky will be different each season. Also, there is the circumpolar region where the stars are visible all year.

This chapter is separated into six sections or "skies." There is one section for each season and one for the northern circumpolar region. The sixth section includes the Southern Hemisphere's constellations.

Early in the evening, you can generally see a few constellations from the previous season (before they set). If you stay up late, you will begin to see constellations from the next season rising in the east.

This book will feature only the most prominent constellations, the ones that will help you learn your way around the night sky.

Circumpolar Constellations

Star map for pages 26–31.

Draco

Cepheus

Ursa Major
(Great Bear)

Ursa Minor
(Little Bear)

North Star

Cassiopeia

Camelopardalis

Pro Tip
Even though this binocular symbol is included for the deep-sky objects, many of these objects can be viewed with the unaided eye from dark skies.

Looking North

If you live at northern latitudes, these stars are visible all year long.

Circumpolar Asterisms

Asterisms for stars on the facing page.

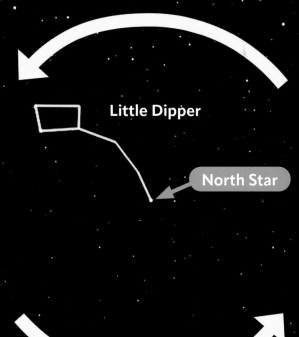

Direction of sky rotation

Little Dipper

North Star

Big Dipper

Big W

Direction of sky rotation

Looking North

Asterisms are recognizable star patterns that are often not associated with the official constellations. Sometimes they include a piece of the constellation, like the **Big Dipper**.

The Big Bear (Ursa Major)

In Greek mythology, a nymph (forest maiden) and her son were turned into two bears by the goddess Hera. These stars are far more famous for the **Big Dipper** and **Little Dipper** asterisms.

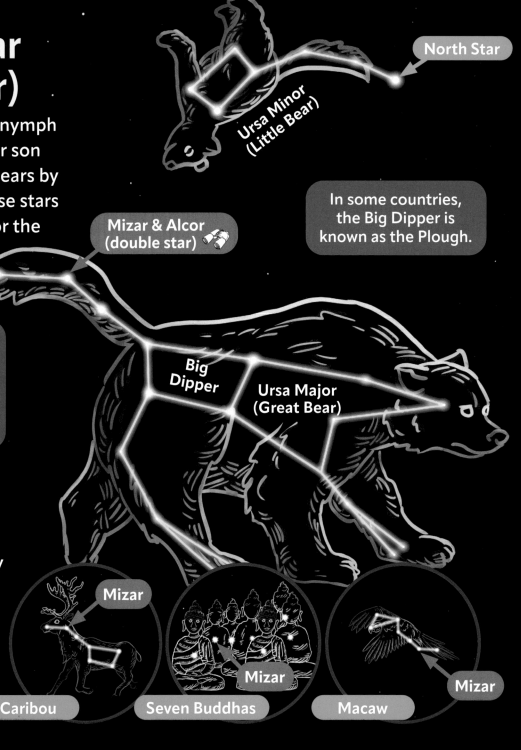

Ursa Minor (Little Bear)

North Star

Mizar & Alcor (double star)

In some countries, the Big Dipper is known as the Plough.

It is interesting that these stars were chosen to represent bears since bears have such short tails, and these patterns have long tails.

Big Dipper

Ursa Major (Great Bear)

These stars represent something different in many cultures. For the Inuit of the North, they represent a **caribou**. In Mongolia, they are **seven Buddhas**, and for the Mayan people, a **macaw**.

Mizar

Mizar

Mizar

Caribou

Seven Buddhas

Macaw

The Little Bear (Ursa Minor)

As well as representing the Little Bear, these same stars also form the asterism known as the Little Dipper.

The Little Dipper is a great way to measure the darkness of your sky. If you can see all four stars in the square, then your skies are reasonably dark. If you cannot see these stars, then you may need to go to darker skies to observe some of the dimmer objects mentioned in this book.

Big Dipper

The entire sky appears to rotate around the North Star about every twenty-four hours.

Ursa Minor (Little Bear/ Little Dipper)

Pherkad (double star)

North Star (aka Polaris)

27

The Giraffe
(Camelopardalis)

Camelopardalis is located in a part of the sky without any bright stars. This part of the sky contains no ancient Greek constellations. In fact, for most cultures, this part of the sky contains no star lore at all!

In the early 1600s, the Giraffe was added. This is what is known as a "modern" constellation as it is not directly associated with ancient myths.

North Star

Kemble's Cascade

Kemble's Cascade as viewed through binoculars

Cassiopeia

Cassiopeia is named for a queen in Greek mythology. To stargazers, this constellation appears as a big **W** or a big **M** depending on the season and time of night.

This is one of the most easily identifiable patterns in the night sky and is found in the myths of many cultures. For the Pima tribe in Arizona, it is a **spider**. In Scandinavia, it represents **antlers**. For some island and coastal cultures, it is a **whale** or **fish tail**, and in the Middle East, it is a **camel**.

Shedar

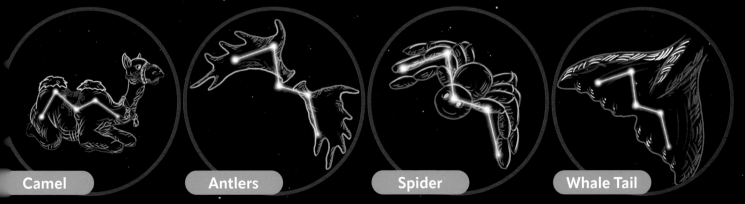

Camel

Antlers

Spider

Whale Tail

29

The Dragon (Draco)

This huge constellation of mostly dim stars fills the space between the **Big Dipper** and the **Summer Triangle** (page XX). The stars that make up the dragon's head are the easiest to identify.

Draco is a dragon in Greek mythology. In Hindu tradition, these same stars form a **dolphin**. For the Dakota tribe in North America, some of these stars form a **thunderbird**.

Vega

Eltanin

Eta Draconis

Thuban

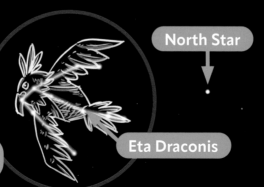

Thunderbird (Dakota)

Eta Draconis

North Star

The celestial poles shift due to Earth's **precession**. During the construction of the Egyptian pyramids, forty-five hundred years ago, Thuban was the North Star.

The King (Cepheus)

In Greek mythology, King Cepheus is the husband of Queen Cassiopeia.

Near the "face" of Cepheus is one of the reddest stars in our sky, known as **the Garnet Star**. This is one of the largest known stars, millions of times the volume of our Sun. It is also a variable star, which changes in brightness over a period of about two years.

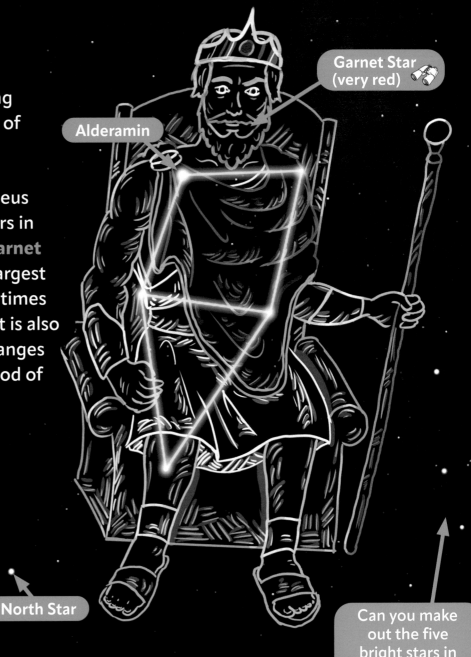

Garnet Star (very red)

Alderamin

If you're having trouble locating this constellation, go back to page 24. Circumpolar constellations can be found on any side of the North Star.

North Star

Can you make out the five bright stars in

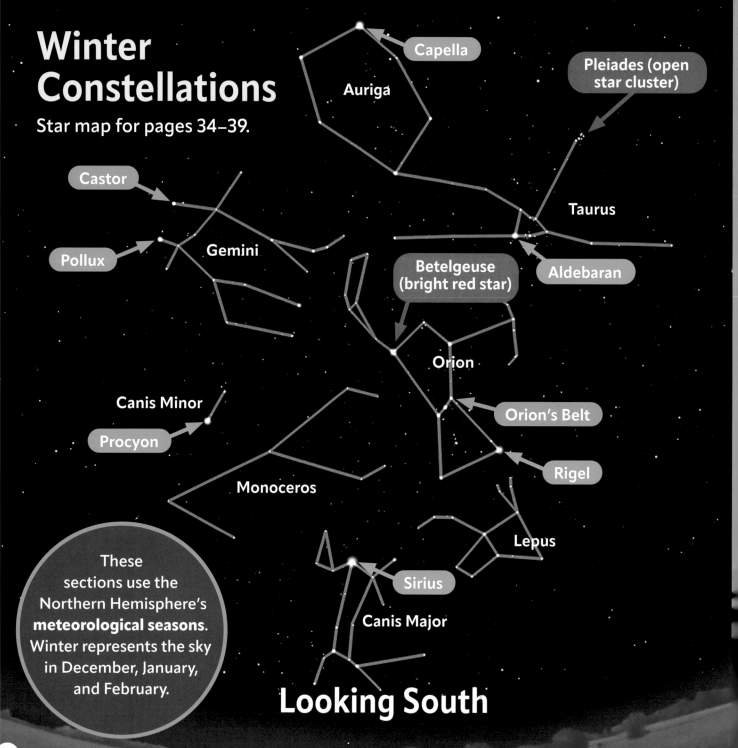

Winter Constellations

Star map for pages 34–39.

Capella

Auriga

Pleiades (open star cluster)

Castor

Pollux

Gemini

Taurus

Betelgeuse (bright red star)

Aldebaran

Orion

Canis Minor

Orion's Belt

Procyon

Rigel

Monoceros

Lepus

These sections use the Northern Hemisphere's **meteorological seasons**. Winter represents the sky in December, January, and February.

Sirius

Canis Major

Looking South

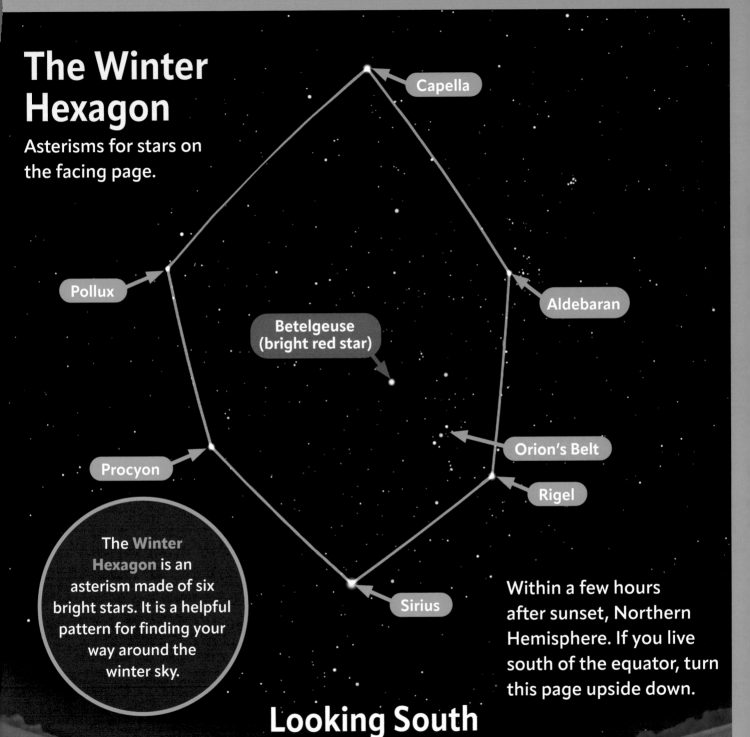

The Winter Hexagon

Asterisms for stars on the facing page.

Capella

Pollux

Aldebaran

Betelgeuse
(bright red star)

Orion's Belt

Procyon

Rigel

The **Winter Hexagon** is an asterism made of six bright stars. It is a helpful pattern for finding your way around the winter sky.

Sirius

Within a few hours after sunset, Northern Hemisphere. If you live south of the equator, turn this page upside down.

Looking South

Orion

Orion is a great hunter in Greek mythology. The constellation is known for the three bright stars in a row known as Orion's Belt. There is a bright red star in Orion's shoulder, Betelgeuse, and a bluish star in his foot, Rigel.

Most cultures see this star pattern as a man or giant. In Hindu culture, he is a cruel father; for Tibetans, a hunchback. In Egypt, he is Osiris, god of the Underworld. And in Mesopotamia, he is the "True Shepherd of the Heavens."

Notice how Orion pursues the Bull across the night sky.

Betelgeuse

Orion Nebula

Orion's Belt

Rigel

Rigel

Betelgeuse

In Hawaiian star lore, these stars are known as the Cat's Cradle, a game that is played with string.

Nebulas are clouds of gas and dust in space. They come in many types. Some are the remains of dying stars, while others are regions where new stars are formed.

Orion Nebula in binoculars

The Bull (Taurus)

This constellation represented a bull even before the Greek myths. There are even cave paintings in France with this constellation represented as a bull.

For the Mayans, these stars represent an owl, and for the Inuit, the Hyades star cluster represents a pack of dogs.

This constellation includes two star clusters visible without binoculars, the Hyades and the Pleiades.

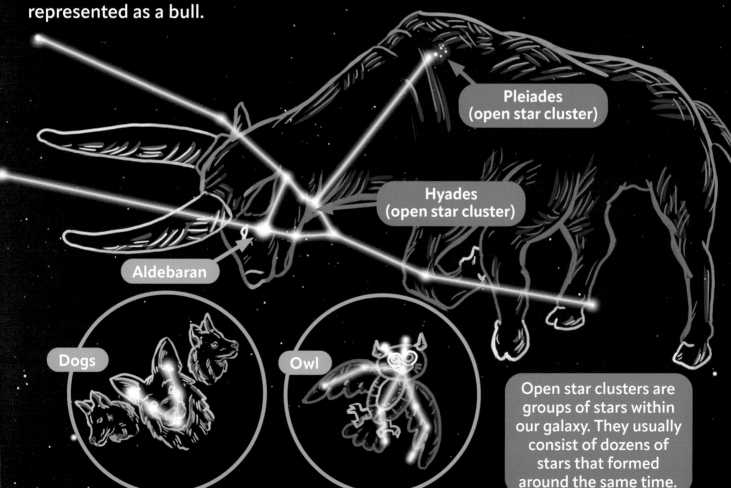

Pleiades (open star cluster)

Hyades (open star cluster)

Aldebaran

Dogs

Owl

Open star clusters are groups of stars within our galaxy. They usually consist of dozens of stars that formed around the same time.

The Greater Dog (Canis Major)

Canis Major is a great dog in Greek mythology. In star lore, this constellation represents several dogs, including Orion's hunting dog.

The bright star in the dog's neck is Sirius, the brightest star in the night sky.

The Boorong of Australia see Sirius as the eye of Warepil, a wedge-tailed eagle, while the dog's hind becomes a jacky lizard.

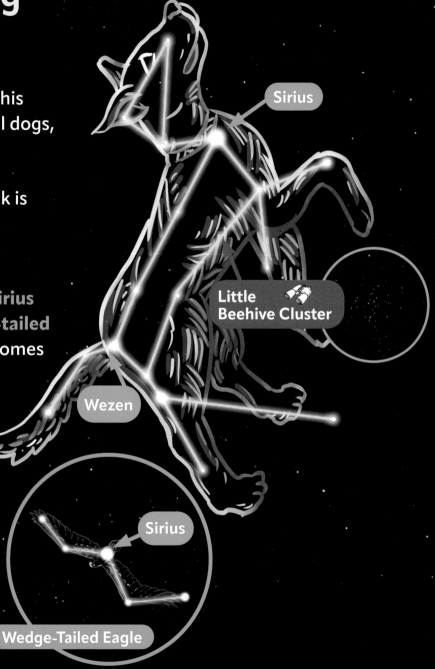

Sirius

Little Beehive Cluster

Wezen

Wezen

Jacky Lizard

Sirius

Wedge-Tailed Eagle

The Hare (Lepus)

This constellation represents a hare. It rises just before the Great Dog (Canis Major) and, just as in the myths, is pursued by the dog across the sky in a never-ending chase.

In ancient Babylonian culture more than two thousand years ago, these stars represented a rooster.

Orion's Belt

Rigel

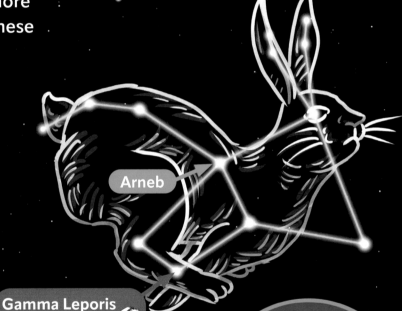

Arneb

Sirius

Arneb

In ancient Chinese and Korean cultures, these stars represented a toilet.

Gamma Leporis (double star)

Did You Know?
Hares are larger than rabbits and change their color in the winter. Hares are also faster!

The Twins (Gemini)

In Greek mythology, Gemini represents twins **Pollux** and **Castor**. The stars representing the heads of the twins bear their names.

For the Boorong of Australia, **Castor** and **Pollux** are Yurree and Wanjel (a **fan-tailed cuckoo** and a **long-necked tortoise**) who hunt Purra the kangaroo. Their appearance in the sky coincides with the life cycles of these animals.

Pollux

Castor

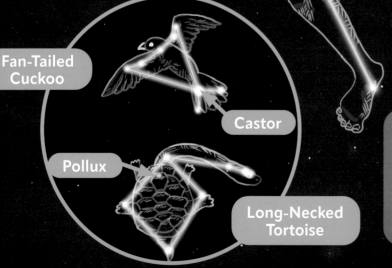

Fan-Tailed Cuckoo

Castor

Pollux

Long-Necked Tortoise

M35 (open cluster)

The names of most deep-sky objects you can see from your backyard start with M followed by a number. M stands for Charles Messier, a French astronomer. The number represents the object's place in his catalog.

The Shepherd (Auriga)

Auriga represents a charioteer in Greek mythology, but most images of this figure are of a shepherd. The brightest star in this constellation, Capella, is visible for most of the year from northern latitudes.

For the Boorong tribe in Australia, the stars surrounding Capella form a red kangaroo that rises in the northeast and quickly falls below the horizon just a few hours later.

There are several star clusters within Auriga visible with binoculars that are a lot of fun to explore.

M37
(open cluster)

Capella

Capella

Red
Kangaroo

M37

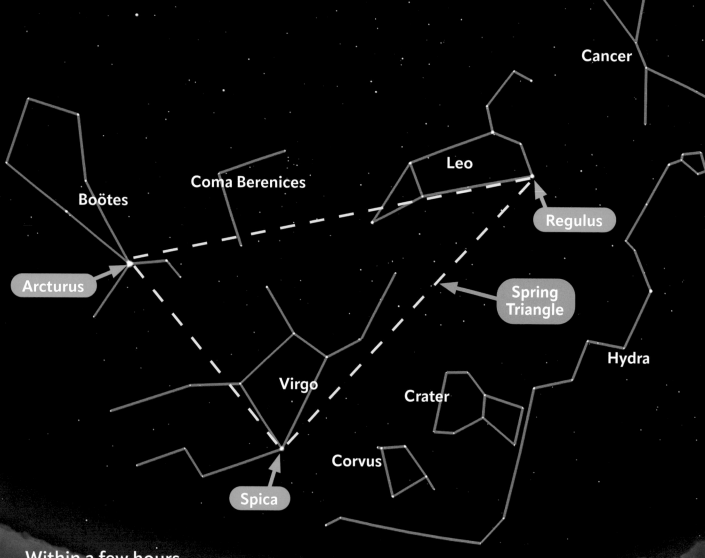

Spring Constellations

Star map for pages 41–45.

Cancer

Coma Berenices

Leo

Boötes

Regulus

Arcturus

Spring Triangle

Virgo

Hydra

Crater

Corvus

Spica

Within a few hours after sunset, Northern Hemisphere.

Looking South

The Lion (Leo)

Leo is the easiest constellation to find in the springtime sky. In many cultures and in Greek mythology, these stars represent a great lion. In others, Leo represents a horse or a panther. The reverse question mark pattern that forms Leo's head is an asterism known as **the Sickle**.

For the Taulipang tribe of Brazil, some of these stars make up the **god of thunder, Tauna**.

Adhafera (double star)

The Sickle

Regulus

Denebola

Tauna, god of thunder

Adhafera is an optical double star, which means that it is not actually orbiting its companion, 35 Leonis.

The Crab (Cancer)

Cancer, **the Crab**, is a very dim constellation and a challenge to see from inside a city or town since it does not contain any bright stars. In Tibet, these stars represent a **frog**, and in ancient Egypt, they were seen as a **tortoise**.

From dark skies, a cluster of stars called **the Beehive** is visible in the center of the constellation.

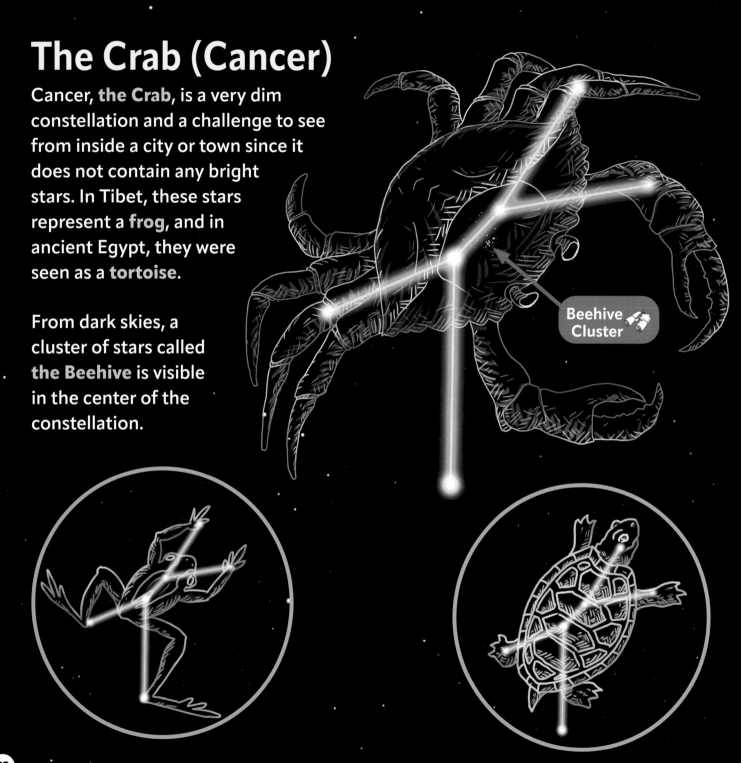

Beehive Cluster

The Herdsman (Boötes)

This constellation is shaped like a giant ice cream cone. The bright red star **Arcturus** is found at its base.

Images of **the Herdsman** often include a sickle (a farming tool) in the left hand. This may be because some of the myths include the harvesting of grapes for wine, and the sickle was used for pruning grapevines.

In the mythologies of several cultures, these stars represent a shepherd (herdsman), but for the Boorong tribe in Australia, these stars represent a giant **meat ant**!

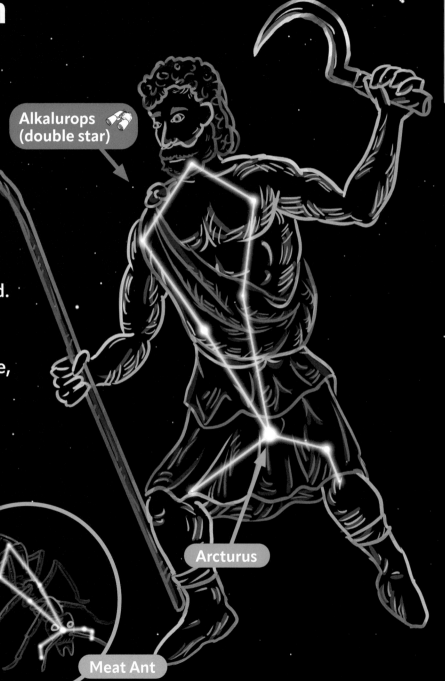

Alkalurops (double star)

Arcturus

Meat Ant

Virgo

The constellation Virgo represents a goddess in many cultures. In Greek mythology, she is a goddess of justice. For the Mayan tribes of Central America, she is a goddess of the Moon, while Christian traditions associate these stars with the Virgin Mary.

The brightest star in this constellation is **Spica**. This part of the sky is popular for those with large telescopes and dark skies, as it is teeming with galaxies!

Spica

Virgo is also the goddess of the harvest.

The Crow and the Cup (Corvus and Crater)

Corvus is a messenger crow or raven in Greek mythology. According to the myths, the crow was sent to collect water in the cup (Crater) for the god Apollo. However, the crow failed in his mission and was placed in the sky as punishment.

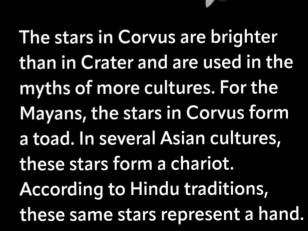

Crater

Corvus

Kraz

The stars in Corvus are brighter than in Crater and are used in the myths of more cultures. For the Mayans, the stars in Corvus form a toad. In several Asian cultures, these stars form a chariot. According to Hindu traditions, these same stars represent a hand.

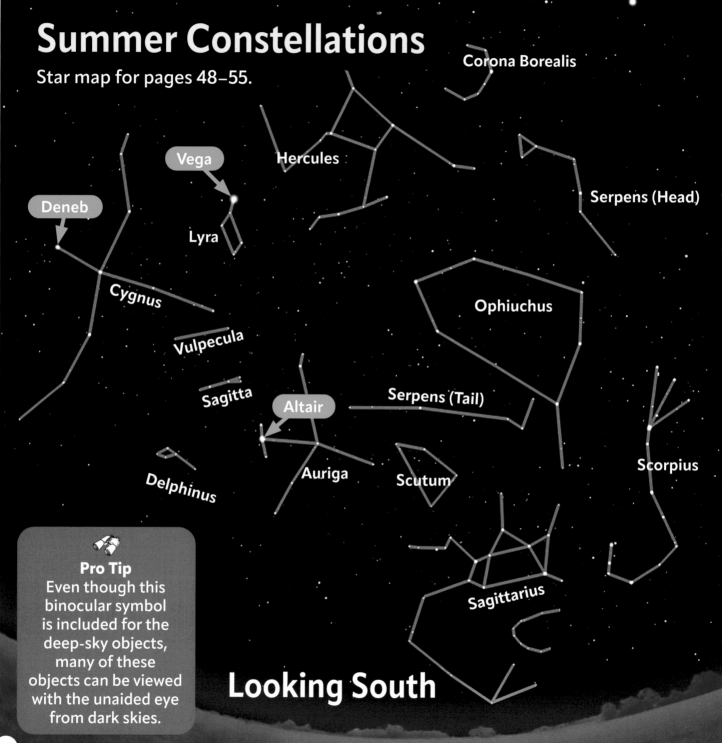

Summer Constellations

Star map for pages 48–55.

Corona Borealis

Vega

Deneb

Hercules

Lyra

Serpens (Head)

Cygnus

Ophiuchus

Vulpecula

Sagitta

Serpens (Tail)

Altair

Delphinus

Auriga

Scutum

Scorpius

Sagittarius

Looking South

Summer Asterisms

Asterisms for stars on the facing page.

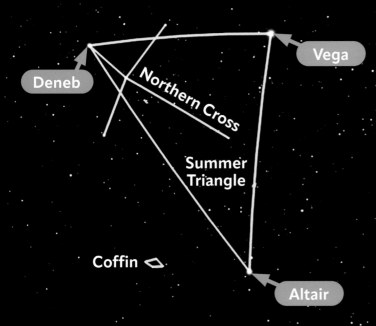

Keystone

Vega

Deneb

Northern Cross

Summer Triangle

Coffin

Altair

Antares (bright red star)

Teapot

Fishhook

Looking South

Hercules

This constellation is named for the Greek hero Hercules, son of Zeus, who was known for his great strength. Stories of Hercules's adventures include fighting monsters and traveling to the underworld.

This small constellation is Corona Borealis, which means Northern Crown.

The four stars in the center of the constellation form an asterism known as **the Keystone.**

This constellation is home to one of the most famous deep-sky objects, globular cluster M13. This cluster can be seen from dark skies with just your eyes as a tiny smudge. Large telescopes reveal thousands of stars.

Globular star clusters are tight groupings of hundreds of thousands of stars. These orbit our galaxy in a region called the **halo**. They appear as tiny smudges when observed without a telescope from a dark location.

Rasalgethi

Alphecca

The Keystone

Vega

M13 globular cluster

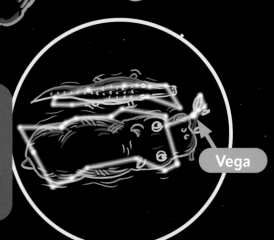

In Egyptian sky culture, these stars form part of a giant alligator and hippopotamus.

Vega

The Fox, the Arrow, and the Dolphin (Vulpecula, Sagitta, and Delphinus)

These tiny constellations are easy to find if you can identify the Summer Triangle (see page 47).

In Greek mythology, the dolphin was a messenger for Poseidon, god of the sea.

Arrows appear in many places in Greek mythology, but it's probably called **the Arrow** because it looks very much like an arrow!

The Fox is the dimmest of the three and is often displayed with a goose in its mouth.

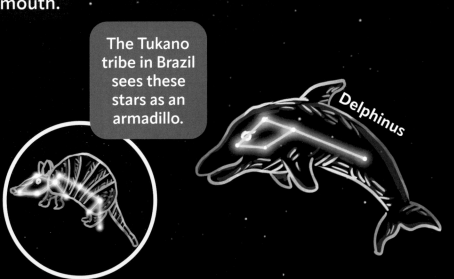

Anser (double star)

Vulpecula

Coat Hanger (asterism)

Sagitta

This is a great part of the sky to explore with binoculars. A small globular cluster resides in the middle of the arrow, and an asterism known as **the Coat Hanger** is found nearby.

The Tukano tribe in Brazil sees these stars as an armadillo.

Delphinus

The Swan (Cygnus)

This constellation resides in a very busy part of the sky. Cygnus is part of the **Summer Triangle**, and the Milky Way runs right through it. There is a lot to see here from a dark sky with or without binoculars.

The body of the Swan forms an asterism called the **Northern Cross**, with the bright star **Deneb** at the top and a famous gold-blue double star called **Albireo** at the bottom.

In Mongolian tradition, these same stars form a bow and arrow!

For the Dakota tribe, the stars of the Northern Cross represent a salamander!

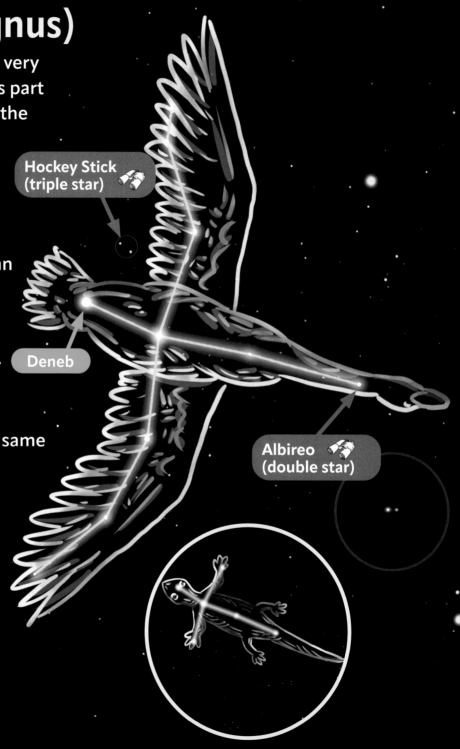

Hockey Stick (triple star)

Deneb

Albireo (double star)

The Harp (Lyra)

This may be a simple constellation, but it's a busy little place. The bright star Vega is the fifth brightest star in the night sky and forms one corner of the Summer Triangle. In Arabic traditions, these stars form a turtle.

There are lots of double stars in Lyra. The most famous is the Double Double (Epsilon Lyra). It is a double star in binoculars, but each star is a double star again in a telescope.

This is also the location of the famous Ring Nebula. A telescope is required to see this object. Binoculars are simply not powerful enough.

Double Double (double star)

Vega

Vega was once the North Star and will be again in twelve thousand years due to precession.

Delta Lyra (double star)

The Ring Nebula (M57) photographed by the Hubble Space Telescope

The Eagle (Aquila)

These stars represent an eagle in Greek mythology. This giant bird was tasked with carrying thunderbolts for Zeus.

The bright star **Altair** is the final star in the **Summer Triangle**.

This part of the sky is very dense with stars. With binoculars under dark skies, you should be able to find the **Wild Duck Cluster**, which looks like a tiny square of stars.

These stars in Aquila are represented as different birds in other cultures: in Persian tradition, a **falcon**; for Australians, a **lorikeet**.

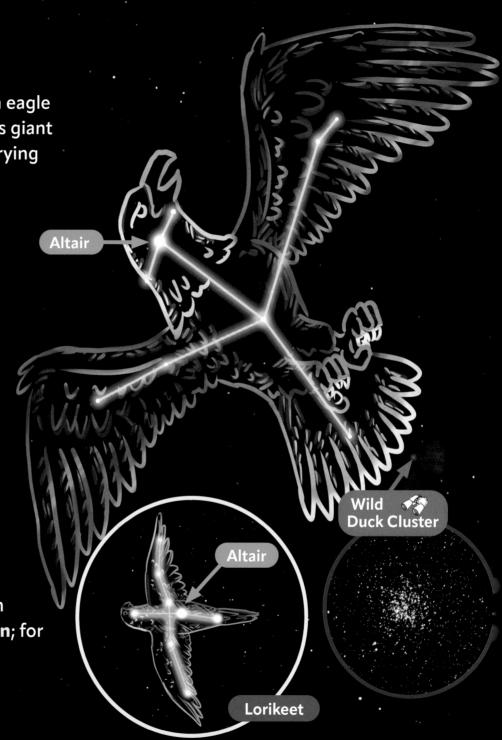

Altair

Altair

Wild Duck Cluster

Lorikeet

The Serpent Holder (Ophiuchus)

Ophiuchus is a large constellation but contains few bright stars. This Greek myth is about a healer who used the power of a magic snake to raise the dead.

Rasalhague

Summer Beehive (star cluster)

The Snake (Serpens)

The constellation Serpens surrounds the constellation Ophiuchus. Some star lore, such as Romanian, only has the snake and ignores Ophiuchus altogether.

The Thirteenth Zodiac Constellation

Ophiuchus is one of the thirteen constellations that our Sun passes through during the year. This makes it a zodiac constellation, at least according to astronomers.

The Archer (Sagittarius)

The core of the Milky Way runs through Sagittarius, making it one of the busiest parts of the sky.

For those living at northern latitudes, this constellation doesn't rise very high. The bottom of the constellation may never rise above your horizon.

The easiest way to find your way around is to use the Teapot asterism. A second asterism known as the Milk Dipper has the star Nunki where the handle meets the cup.

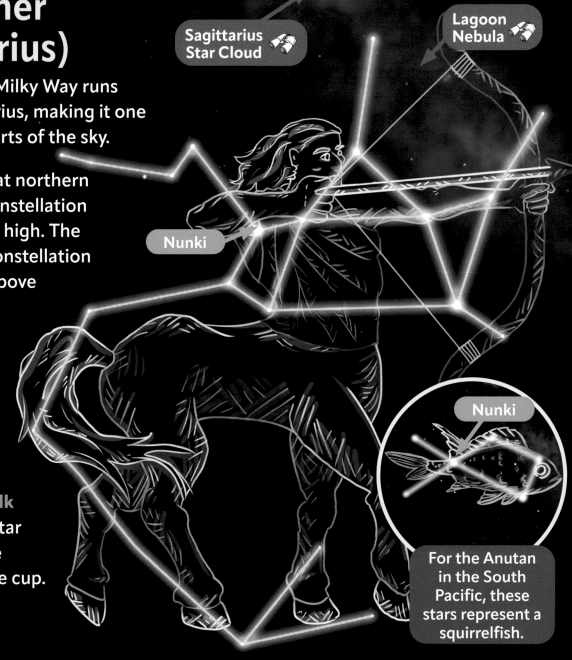

Sagittarius Star Cloud

Lagoon Nebula

Nunki

Nunki

For the Anutan in the South Pacific, these stars represent a squirrelfish.

The Scorpion (Scorpius)

Scorpius is another constellation that's low on the horizon for those living in the north. Its clawlike shape makes it easy to identify.

The bright red star at the base of the claw is **Antares**. This star is often confused with Mars, which sometimes appears in the same part of the sky.

In Hawaiian star lore, these stars make up **Maui's Fishhook**, and for the Boorong in Australia, the stars in the claw form a **red-rumped parrot**.

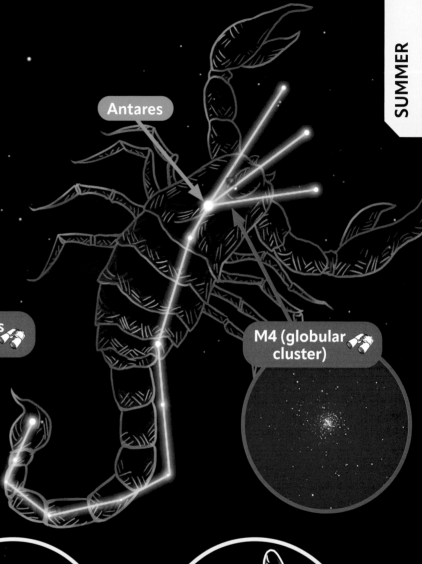

Antares

Ptolemy's Cluster

M4 (globular cluster)

Antares

Red-Rumped Parrot

Maui's Fishhook

Autumn Constellations

Star map for pages 58–63.

Cassiopeia

Mirfak

Andromeda Galaxy

Perseus

Andromeda

Triangulum

Aries

Pegasus

Pisces

Aquarius

Cetus

Piscis Austrinus

Within a few hours after sunset, Northern Hemisphere.

Looking South

Autumn Asterisms

Asterisms for stars on the facing page.

Great Square of Pegasus

Head of the Whale (in Cetus)

Circlet (in Pisces)

Binoculars Tips

When stargazing with binoculars, find your target's location by eye first. Then, slowly bring the binoculars up to your face. If you're having trouble, cover one of the lenses, but keep both eyes open.

Looking South

Perseus

Perseus is named for a Greek hero who is famous for killing the gorgon Medusa. A gorgon is a mythological monster with snakes for hair.

For the Tukano of Brazil, these stars (along with the stars in Cassiopeia) represent a jaguar.

The brightest star is called Mirfak. Between Perseus and Cassiopeia is a deep-sky object called the Double Cluster, two star clusters visible without a telescope in dark skies.

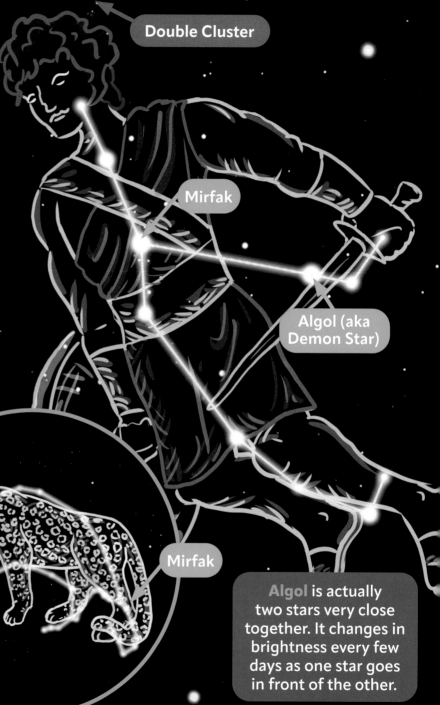

Double Cluster

Mirfak

Algol (aka Demon Star)

Mirfak

Jaguar

Algol is actually two stars very close together. It changes in brightness every few days as one star goes in front of the other.

Pegasus

This is one of the most prominent star patterns in the autumn sky. Pegasus is a winged horse in Greek mythology. The Great Square is an asterism composed of the four stars in the body of the horse.

For the Lakota in North America, the Great Square represents a turtle named Keya. For the Ojibwa, it is the Great Moose, and its rising marks the beginning of moose hunting season.

Globular cluster M15 will appear as a tiny smudge in dark skies.

M15 (globular cluster)

Markab

Alpheratz (this star is part of Andromeda too)

Great Moose

Turtle

Andromeda

In Greek mythology, Andromeda was the daughter of Queen Cassiopeia (page 29). She was chained to a rock to be eaten by the sea monster Cetus. Perseus and Pegasus saved Andromeda before that could happen.

For the Navajo in North America, the stars in this part of the sky represent a lizard.

The star Mirach is used as a reference for finding the Andromeda Galaxy. Almach is one of the most beautiful double stars in the sky. Even with a small telescope, one star will appear gold, the other a bright blue.

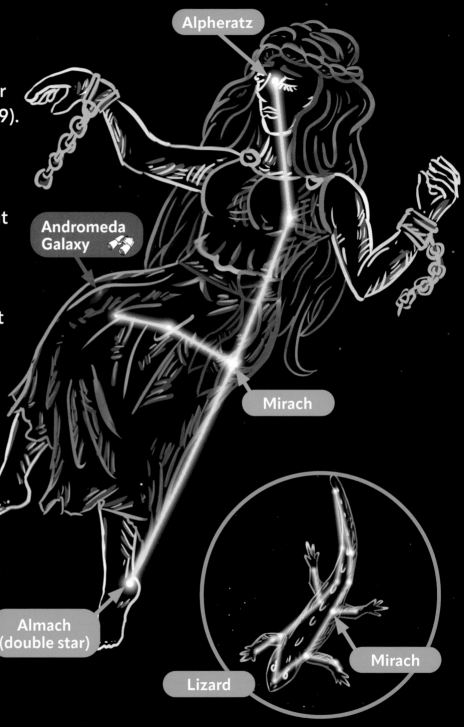

Alpheratz

Andromeda Galaxy 🔭

Mirach

Almach (double star)

Lizard

Mirach

The Whale (Cetus)

Cetus is a sea monster in Greek mythology. This constellation is often called **the Whale**. Its most prominent feature is the hexagon of stars that make up the whale's head.

Cetus is very challenging to see from the city. Its brightest star is **Menkar**, located in the asterism called **the Head of the Whale**.

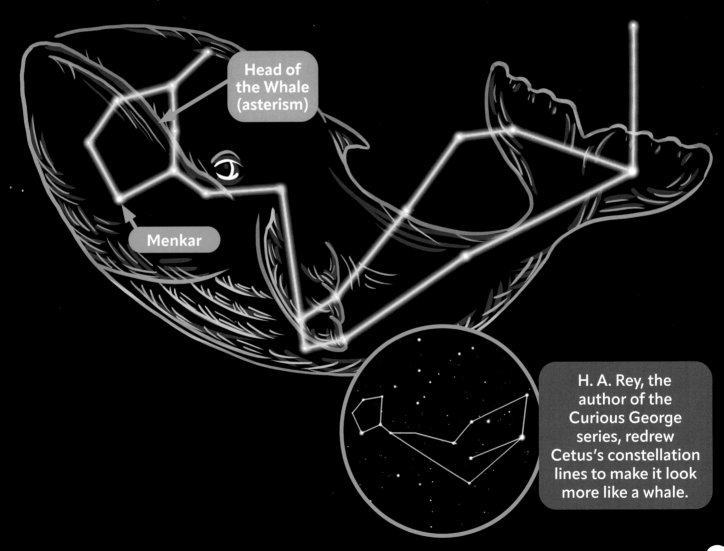

Head of the Whale (asterism)

Menkar

H. A. Rey, the author of the Curious George series, redrew Cetus's constellation lines to make it look more like a whale.

The Water Carrier (Aquarius)

Aquarius is a constellation of dim stars. It is not a very popular target for stargazing. However, Aquarius does contain a popular target for binoculars and small telescopes, a globular cluster called M2.

In Greek mythology, Aquarius is a mortal servant who brings water to the gods.

South of Aquarius is the star Fomalhaut, one of the brightest stars in the sky. This star is part of a constellation named Piscis Austrinus.

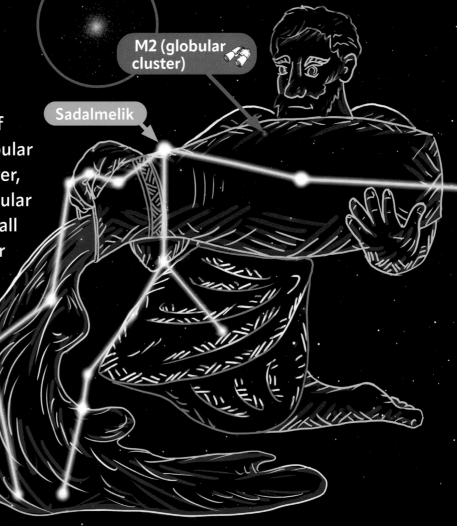

M2 (globular cluster)

Sadalmelik

Fomalhaut

The Sun enters Aquarius in mid-February and leaves in mid-March, making it a zodiac constellation.

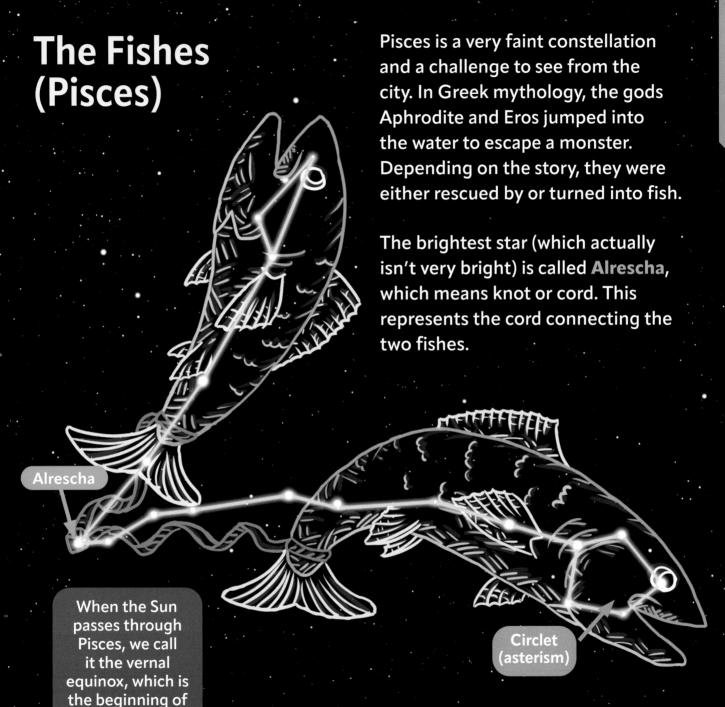

The Fishes (Pisces)

Pisces is a very faint constellation and a challenge to see from the city. In Greek mythology, the gods Aphrodite and Eros jumped into the water to escape a monster. Depending on the story, they were either rescued by or turned into fish.

The brightest star (which actually isn't very bright) is called **Alrescha**, which means knot or cord. This represents the cord connecting the two fishes.

Alrescha

When the Sun passes through Pisces, we call it the vernal equinox, which is the beginning of spring!

Circlet (asterism)

Southern Hemisphere Constellations

Star map for pages 65–67.

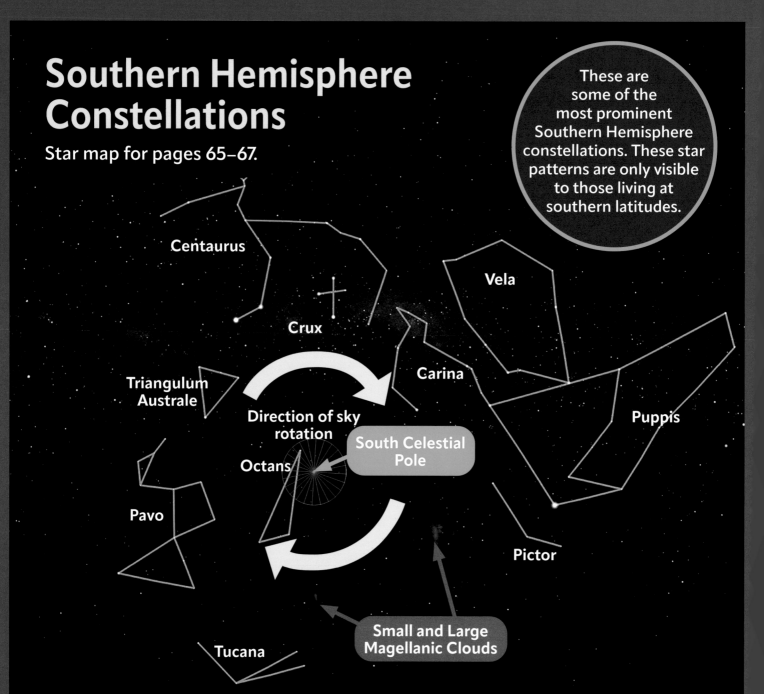

These are some of the most prominent Southern Hemisphere constellations. These star patterns are only visible to those living at southern latitudes.

Centaurus

Vela

Crux

Carina

Triangulum Australe

Puppis

Direction of sky rotation

South Celestial Pole

Octans

Pavo

Pictor

Tucana

Small and Large Magellanic Clouds

Looking South

The Ship (Vela, Carina, and Puppis)

The Ship was once considered a single constellation known as the Argo Navis, from Greek mythology.

If you live in the southern part of the Northern Hemisphere (Mexico or Florida, for example), the Ship will rise above the horizon (briefly) in early spring.

Sail (Vela)

Great Nebula in Carina

Poop Deck (Puppis)

Keel (Carina)

The plane of the Milky Way runs right through the Ship. There are dozens of star clusters to explore here with binoculars.

Canopus

The Centaur and the Southern Cross (Centaurus and Crux)

The Southern Cross, or Crux, is the most famous constellation for those living at southern latitudes. These four bright stars helped ancient voyagers find islands, like Hawaii, in the middle of the Pacific Ocean.

The bright star in the Centaur's leg is **Alpha Centauri**, the closest star system to our Sun (at only forty-one trillion kilometers away). It would take about eighty thousand years to travel this distance at about sixty thousand kilometers per hour.

Jewel Box Cluster

Alpha Centauri

Acrux (double star)

The Peacock, the Toucan, and the Octant (Pavo, Tucana, and Octans)

There are several small constellations near the South Celestial Pole. These constellations are **circumpolar** for those living in places like Australia, Argentina, and South Africa.

The South Celestial Pole is located within the boundaries of the constellation Octans (remember, a constellation is a region of sky, not the lines themselves).

Tucana contains one of the brightest globular clusters, known as 47 Tuc. It is found right next to the Small Magellanic Cloud.

The bright star in Pavo (the Peacock) also goes by the name Peacock.

Triangulum Australe

Pavo

Peacock

Octans

47 Tuc (globular cluster)

Tucana

South Celestial Pole

Small Magellanic Cloud

Chapter 4

Astronomical Events

Our night sky is a busy place! Every few weeks, there is an interesting event occurring. Whether it's a meteor shower, a supermoon, or a comet, there's almost always something to look forward to.

Earth's shadow

Lunar Eclipse

A lunar eclipse occurs during a full moon when the Moon enters Earth's shadow. We don't get a lunar eclipse every full moon because the Moon's orbit around Earth is tilted by five degrees. Most months, the Moon misses Earth's shadow entirely!

Blood Moon

When the Moon enters Earth's shadow during an eclipse, it still receives some light from the Sun, but that light has passed through Earth's atmosphere, giving the Moon its red color!

Meteor Showers

Meteors, also known as shooting stars, are tiny space rocks entering Earth's atmosphere. They travel so fast they burn up due to friction, and we see them as streaks of light across the sky.

There are many meteor showers every year, but they can be a challenge to observe. You must be far away from city lights, and you want the peak of the meteor shower to occur on an evening when the Moon is not in the sky.

Meteors can often be traced back to a certain part of the sky or constellation. This is where meteor showers get their names. You do not need to look at this part of the sky in particular to enjoy the shower.

Fireballs

Fireballs, also called bolides, are meteors that are extremely bright. Sometimes, these space rocks explode and can even make noise that can be heard from the ground!

Meteoroid

A small rock in space.

Meteor

A streak of light caused by a space rock that has entered the atmosphere.

Meteorite

A space rock that has hit the ground.

Meteor Shower Dates

Meteor shower	(approximate) peak.
Quadrantids	Early January
Lyrids	Late April
Eta Aquariids	Early May
Delta Aquariids	Late July
Perseids	Mid-August
Draconids	Early October
Orionids	Late October
Leonids	Mid-November
Geminids	Mid-December

Meteor Showers

Meteor showers occur when Earth passes through the orbit of a comet or debris from an asteroid.

Despite what you see in pictures (including this long exposure by photographer Craig Taylor), it is rare to see more than one meteor at a time. Most of the time, there are several minutes between each one.

Comets

Comets are city-sized balls of ice and dust that orbit the Sun. Sometimes, comets pass near the Sun and shed their outer layers in a tail of gas and dust.

These tails are millions of kilometers long and can be seen from Earth. Every year, there are a few comets bright enough to be seen in binoculars or a backyard telescope, and sometimes these comets are visible without a telescope at all.

Comet Pan-STARRS viewed without a telescope in March 2013

Rosetta

Comet 67P imaged by the Rosetta spacecraft

Auroras

People who live at far northern latitudes, in dark skies, are treated to an amazing spectacle known as the aurora borealis or northern lights. This display of color in the skies occurs when particles from the Sun interact with gas in Earth's upper atmosphere.

Sometimes, the aurora is quite dim and looks to the eye like distant smoke. Other times, it can appear as if the entire sky is on fire.

In the Southern Hemisphere, this phenomenon is known as the **aurora australis** or southern lights.

73

Satellites

If you look at the stars for more than a few minutes, you will be sure to see a **satellite**. These appear as tiny points of light crossing the entire sky in just a few minutes. Sometimes they suddenly disappear as they enter Earth's shadow. If the light is flashing, you are seeing a high-flying airplane.

Some satellites start dim, then shine extremely bright, and then get dim again. These are called satellite flares. This is caused by giant panels that reflect sunlight like a mirror.

Satellite with bright reflective panel

International Space Station

Some satellites, like the International Space Station (ISS), are incredibly bright. You can download an app that will tell you when the ISS is about to pass overhead.

Conjunctions

Conjunctions occur when objects appear close together in the sky. The Moon has a conjunction with each planet every month during its twenty-seven-day orbit around Earth. Other times, conjunctions occur when two or three planets appear close together.

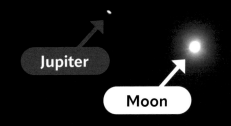

Jupiter

Moon

Venus

Occultations

Occultations occur when a planet or bright star goes behind the Moon. It can be fun to observe the planet disappear on one side of the Moon and then reappear on the other. This is especially impressive with a telescope! However, since the Moon is much smaller than Earth, an occultation is only visible from certain places.

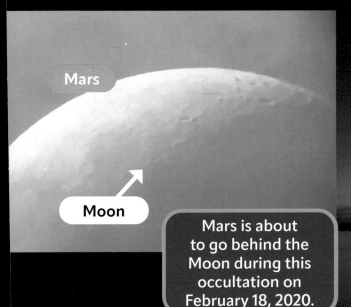

Mars

Moon

Mars is about to go behind the Moon during this occultation on February 18, 2020.

Orbit of Jupiter

Orbit of Saturn

Chapter 5

A Tour of the Solar System

Only Mercury, Venus, Mars, Jupiter, and Saturn can be seen from the city. Under a clear dark sky, it is possible to see Uranus with the unaided eye. Neptune requires binoculars or a telescope.

Planets generally appear brighter than the surrounding stars and appear to change position (some more than others) from night to night.

The Ecliptic

Because planets orbit the Sun in a disk, they always appear along the same path in the sky. This path is known as the **ecliptic**.

Orbit of Mars

Orbit of Venus

Orbit of Mercury

The Sun

Retrograde Motion

If you track a planet's motion across the sky from night to night, sometimes it will appear to move in the opposite direction for several days. This occurs when Earth passes that planet in its orbit. This is what it means for a planet to be in retrograde.

Mercury

The planet Mercury orbits closest to our Sun. It is also the smallest planet in our solar system, only slightly larger than Earth's Moon.

Even though Mercury is the closest to the Sun, it's not the hottest; Venus holds that title due to its thick atmosphere.

Because Mercury is so close to the Sun, it can only be seen in the sky shortly after sunset in the west or shortly before sunrise in the east.

Image of Mercury taken by the MESSENGER spacecraft

The "Closest" Planet

Mercury is not only the closest planet to the Sun. On average, it is the closest planet to all the other planets as well, even Earth! At first, this might not make any sense at all.

But think deeply about this: half the time, planets are on the opposite side of the Sun from one another. This means that Mercury, which is hanging out near the Sun, is, on average, closer to each planet! Does your brain hurt yet?

As of 2022, only two spacecraft have visited Mercury. The first was a spacecraft named Mariner 10, which flew by Mercury in 1974.

A spacecraft named MESSENGER arrived at Mercury in 2011, orbiting the planet for over four years. During this time, the spacecraft created detailed maps of Mercury's surface. It also measured the planet's **magnetic field** and its extremely thin atmosphere (called an **exosphere**).

A third space probe, named BepiColombo will visit Mercury in 2025.

MESSENGER spacecraft

Mercury gets its name from Roman mythology. Mercury was the Roman god of travelers and acted as a messenger. Mercury is the fastest moving planet.

Mercury through a backyard telescope

Venus

Venus is known as Earth's twin. It's almost exactly the same size. However, a cloudy atmosphere made almost entirely of carbon dioxide has created a greenhouse effect so extreme that the surface temperature is almost five hundred degrees Celsius. This makes Venus the hottest planet in the solar system. The pressure on the planet's surface is like being deep in the ocean.

Because Venus is an inner planet like Mercury, it also appears after sunset in the west and before sunrise in the east.

Image of Venus taken by the Mariner 10 spacecraft

Exploration by Blimp

How could humans explore Venus? Well, imagine you filled a giant blimp or airship with breathable air, then put this ship in Venus's atmosphere. It should be possible to position this airship at an altitude where the temperature and pressure would be nearly identical to that of Earth.

Venus was named for the Roman goddess of love and beauty.

There have been dozens of robotic space missions to Venus, stretching back to 1966. The Soviet Union (present-day Russia) landed several spacecraft on the surface, taking amazing photographs along the way.

A spacecraft called Venera 8 became the first human object to land on another planet. This spacecraft was launched by the Soviet Union in 1972, taking just over 100 days to get to Venus. The spacecraft lasted about an hour on the surface before succumbing to the extreme temperatures and pressures.

Venus has phases just like our Moon. This is how Venus appears through a backyard telescope. Because Venus is closer to the Sun than Earth, we sometimes see its nighttime side.

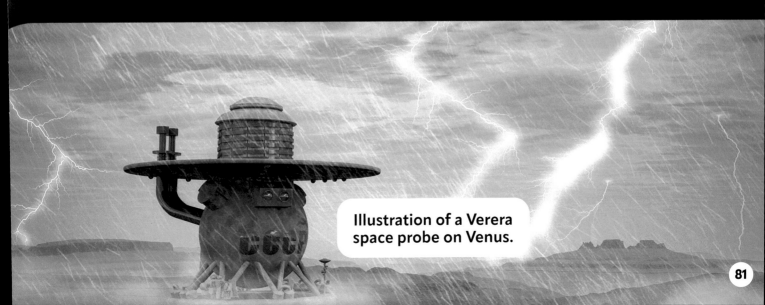

Illustration of a Verera space probe on Venus.

Currently, there are several robots on the surface of Mars. These robots help researchers study the planet's history and look for signs of past and present life-forms.

Mars was named after the Roman god of war.

Humans on Mars

When humans finally land on Mars, they'll need to live in pressurized habitats, under domes, or underground. These structures will protect them from radiation, low air pressure, and extreme cold.

Image of Mars's moon Phobos taken by the Mars Reconnaissance Orbiter

Mars has two moons, Phobos and Deimos. These moons are very small, and cannot be seen with backyard telescopes

Mars's moon Deimos

From Earth, Mars's polar ice caps and different colored soils can be observed using large backyard telescopes.

A Mars rover named Curiosity takes a "selfie" using its robotic arm. Can't see the arm? That's be cause this is actually 11 images stitched together.

Jupiter

As one of the brightest objects in our night sky, Jupiter has fascinated humanity for thousands of years. The discovery of Jupiter's four Galilean moons, with the invention of the telescope in 1609, changed how we viewed the universe forever.

Galileo observed moons orbiting Jupiter following a known set of physical laws. This offered the first proof that Earth orbited the Sun and not the other way around.

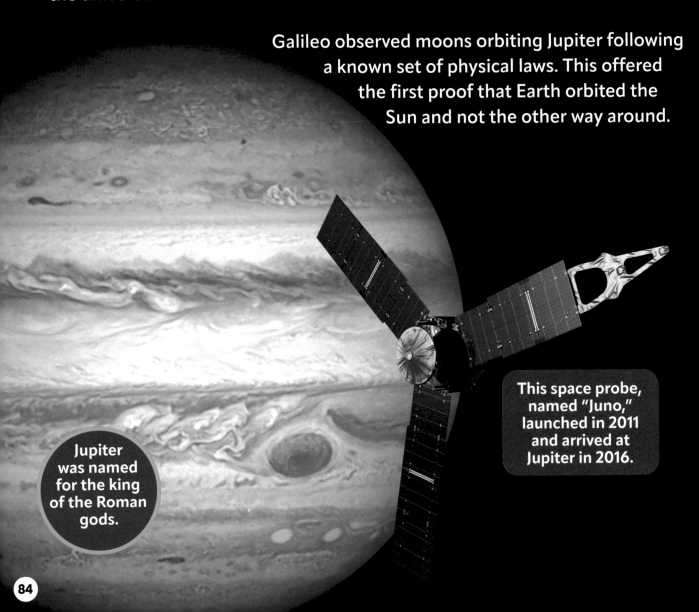

This space probe, named "Juno," launched in 2011 and arrived at Jupiter in 2016.

Jupiter was named for the king of the Roman gods.

Jupiter's Galilean Moons

Jupiter has 79 known moons, but only the four largest moons are easily seen from Earth in binoculars or small telescopes. These moons are named the Galilean moons after Galileo, who was the first to observe them.

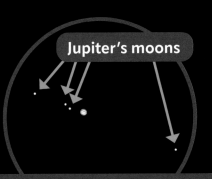

Jupiter's moons

Jupiter and the Galilean moons as they appear in a backyard telescope or binoculars. If you observe the moons from night to night, you can see that they move around Jupiter.

Ganymede is the largest moon in the Solar System.

Europa is the smallest of the four Galilean moons. Beneath an icy surface, there is an ocean of liquid water.

Io hosts more than 400 active volcanoes!

Callisto orbits almost two million kilometers from Jupiter. Through binoculars, it almost looks like a background star.

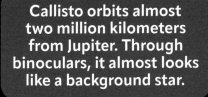

Saturn

Saturn is one of the most beautiful objects in the solar system. For many people, one look at this planet through a telescope is all it takes to become hooked on astronomy for life.

Saturn's rings are made of tiny pieces of ice and rock. They are thought to have been formed by asteroids, comets, and moons torn apart by Saturn's gravity.

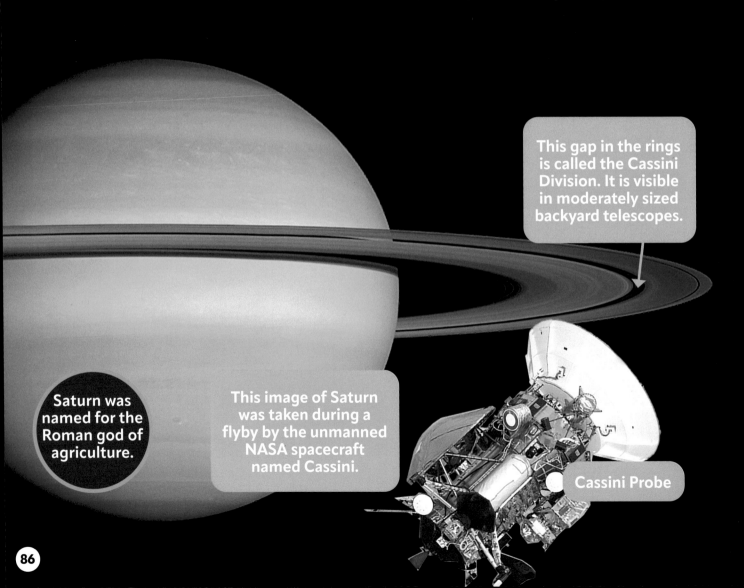

This gap in the rings is called the Cassini Division. It is visible in moderately sized backyard telescopes.

Saturn was named for the Roman god of agriculture.

This image of Saturn was taken during a flyby by the unmanned NASA spacecraft named Cassini.

Cassini Probe

Saturn's Moons

Like Jupiter, Saturn sports dozens of interesting moons. The largest is Titan which is a rocky moon with a thick atmosphere. Many of the other moons are made of ice, and some, like Enceladus, have dozens of geysers that shoot ice up into space.

Saturn and its moons as they would appear through a backyard telescope. On most nights, you should be able to see Saturn's largest moon, Titan. With larger telescopes, you should be able to see several other moons, such as Rhea, Dione, and Tethys.

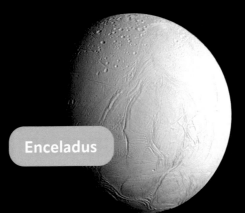

Enceladus

Titan

Titan has a thick atmosphere, and on its surface are lakes of liquid methane. A probe named Huygens parachuted down to the surface and took this photo.

Uranus

Uranus and Neptune are known as the ice giants. They have only been visited by one robotic spacecraft, Voyager 2. The Voyager 2 probe flew past Uranus in 1986 and Neptune in 1989.

Although it is technically possible to see Uranus without a telescope as a tiny point of light in dark skies, it was not discovered until 1781. When astronomer William Herschel first saw the planet, he thought it was a comet.

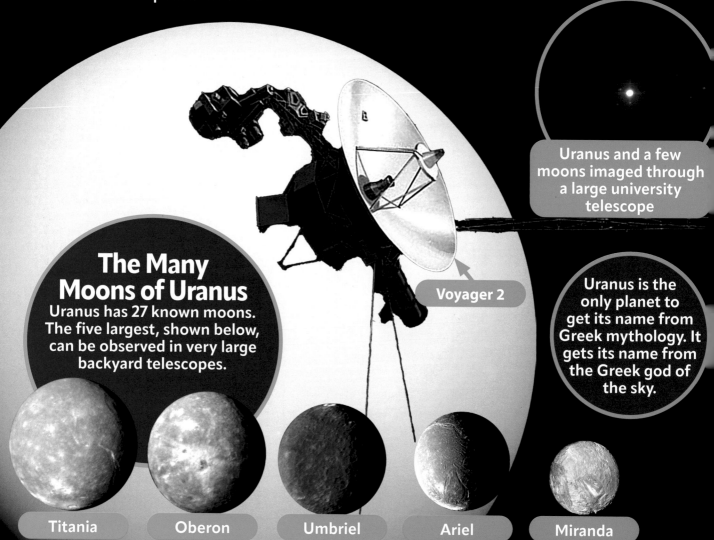

Uranus and a few moons imaged through a large university telescope

Voyager 2

The Many Moons of Uranus

Uranus has 27 known moons. The five largest, shown below, can be observed in very large backyard telescopes.

Uranus is the only planet to get its name from Greek mythology. It gets its name from the Greek god of the sky.

Titania

Oberon

Umbriel

Ariel

Miranda

Neptune

Neptune is the most distant planet in the solar system. It is known for having the strongest winds. Neptune is heavier than Uranus, but it is also smaller than Uranus! How can this be? Neptune's extra mass creates extra gravity, which smushes its gassy body into a smaller volume.

Neptune was named after the Roman god of the sea.

Neptune and Triton as they would appear through a very large backyard telescope

Pro Tip

To see Uranus and Neptune in binoculars (as a point of light) pick a date when they have conjunctions with the Moon or brighter planets or stars.

Image of Neptune's moon Triton taken by the Voyager 2 spacecraft

Pluto is a dwarf planet and part of a "binary planetary system." Pluto and its largest moon, Charon, orbit around a point called a **barycenter**. A barycenter is sort of like the base of a teeter-totter, with the weights perfectly balanced.

Pluto is so distant that if you lived there, our Sun would appear as a very bright star. Pluto is very difficult to identify using backyard telescopes, but it is possible.

Here's an image of Pluto taken with a powerful university telescope. Can you tell which is Pluto? (probably not)

This close-up view of Pluto's mountains and plains was taken during New Horizons' closest approach to the dwarf planet.

Did you know?

Pluto is over 5 billion kilometers from Earth. That's over 5 hours at the speed of light!

Pluto gets its name from the Roman god of the underworld. The name was chosen by an 11-year-old girl named Venetia Burney.

Charon

Charon and Pluto orbit around each other about once each week. Both Pluto and Charon are tidally locked. This means that if you were standing on Pluto, or standing on Charon, the other world would appear in about the same spot all the time!

The robotic New Horizons spacecraft flew past Pluto and Charon in June of 2015

Image of Pluto and Charon together taken by the New Horizons spacecraft, just over 20 million kilometers distant, as it approached the system.

Charon is the name of the ferryman from the underworld in Greek mythology.

Explore the Moon

Earth

Moon

The Moon is, on average, 384,000 kilometers from Earth. This is what the actual distance looks like to scale.

This image is from Apollo 17. It was taken in 1972 during the most recent crewed mission to the Moon.

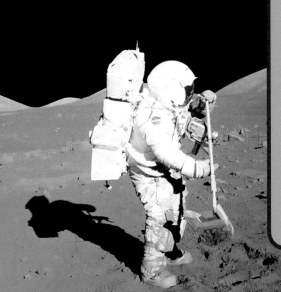

Daytime Moon

Can you see the Moon during the day? Absolutely! For about half the month, the Moon is visible at some point during the day.

For example, at first quarter, the Moon rises at noon and is visible until about midnight.

Moon Facts

- The Moon orbits (goes around) Earth every twenty-seven days.

- The same side of the Moon always faces Earth. This is called **tidal locking**.

- The part of the Moon we cannot see from Earth is called the far side.

- The length of time between two full moons is 29.5 days. This is longer than the Moon's orbit due to Earth's movement around the Sun.

Lunar Activity #1

Use a soccer ball to represent the Moon and a beach ball to represent Earth. Have a friend hold the beach ball. Take the Moon (soccer ball), and take twenty-three big steps (about twenty-three meters, or seventy-five feet) away.

The beach ball will appear as big as Earth as seen from the Moon. Your friend will see the soccer ball appear as big as the Moon does from Earth!

Waxing Lunar Phases

This is how the Moon appears at the same time each evening during the first fourteen days of the lunar cycle.

Day 8

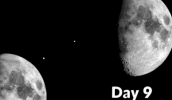

Day 9

Day 10

Day 11

Gibbous Moon

Day 12

Day 13

Day 14

Full Moon

Lunar Activity #2

Place a small foam ball on a toothpick. As the Sun is setting, hold the ball at arm's length, and slowly spin in a circle. Observe the lunar phases as they appear on the ball.

Day 7

First Quarter

Day 6

Day 5

Crescent Moon

Day 4

For the last fourteen days of the lunar cycle, the Moon "wanes" (the light side gets smaller) until it reaches new moon again and the cycle repeats.

Day 3

The transition between the Moon's "day-side" and "night-side" is called the terminator, aka "The Twilight Zone."

Day 2

Young Moon

Day 1

This diagram assumes you are living in the Northern Hemisphere and looking south.

The "New Moon" occurs around day zero when the Moon is nearly in line with the Sun and we cannot see it.

The Moon Up Close

With just your eyes, the Moon never appears any larger than a pea held at arm's length. In fact, you can always cover the Moon with the tip of your pinkie finger.

But even with binoculars or a toy telescope, dozens of amazing features come into view. The type of telescope you are using also affects your view. Some telescopes flip the image left to right, while others appear to turn the image upside down.

Notice where this feature appears in each view.

Binocular (or naked eye) view

Newtonian view (inverted image)

Refractor view with regular diagonal (mirror reversed)

"Big Moon" Illusion

Have you ever seen the full moon rising? It looks huge, doesn't it? But it's not. It's still the size of a pea held at arm's length. The Moon only looks huge because you're seeing it beside familiar objects like trees and buildings.

Craters
There are thousands of craters on the Moon visible with a small telescope. Craters are mainly formed by asteroid or meteoroid impact, but some may be ancient collapsed volcanoes.

Rilles (Cracks), Rupes (Cliffs), and Valles (Valleys)
The Moon is covered in cracks, cliffs, and valleys. These features can be hundreds of kilometers long and several kilometers wide.

Lunar Mountain Ranges
Just like Earth, the Moon has mountains! Most of the Moon's mountains were formed when rock was pushed up by giant asteroid impacts, which means they were formed in a matter of minutes!

Rays
Formed when rock and dust (called ejecta) are dislodged after a meteor impact, lunar rays appear as bright streaks across the lunar surface.

Lunar Seas
Lunar seas (also called *maria*, pronounced "mah-REE-ah") appear as large patches of gray on the Moon's surface. These "seas" were formed from ancient lava flows. Scientists have measured their age at several billion years old.

The Limb
Where the Moon meets the sky.

The Lunar Seas

Binoculars recommended

Sea of Clouds
(Mare Nubium)

Sea of Rains
(Mare Imbrium)

Ocean of Storms
(Oceanus Procellarum)

Known Sea
(Mare Cognitum)

Sea of Moisture
(Mare Humorum)

Sea of Cold
(Mare Frigoris)

Sea of Serenity
(Mare Serenitatis)

Sea of Tranquility
(Mare Tranquillitatis)

Sea of Crises
(Mare Crisium)

Sea of Fertility
(Mare Fecunditatis)

Sea of Vapors
(Mare Vaporum)

Sea of Nectar
(Mare Nectaris)

Lunar Activity #3

During a full moon (or nearly full moon),
identify all the lunar seas. Check the boxes
after you've observed each one.

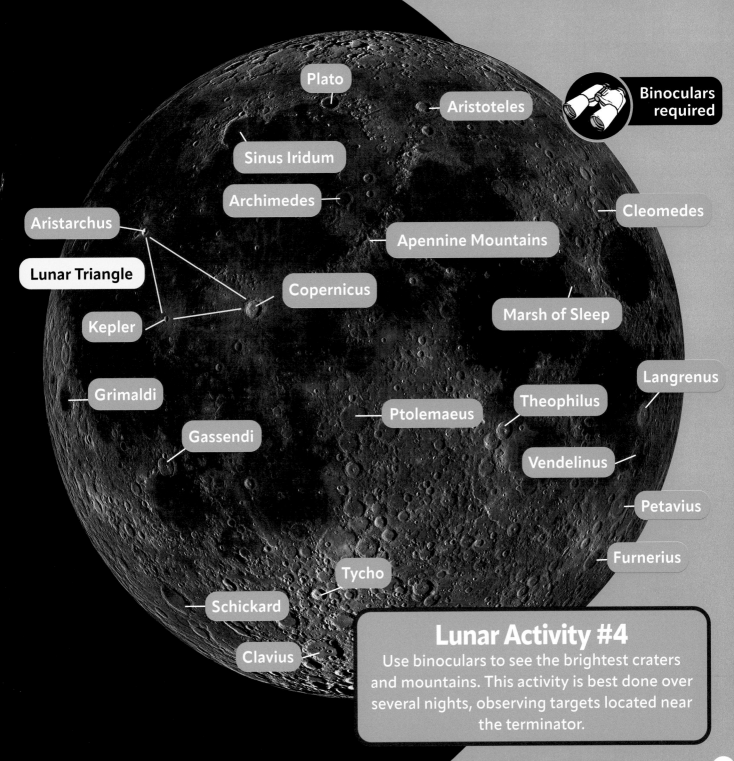

Plato

Aristoteles

Binoculars
required

Sinus Iridum

Cleomedes

Archimedes

Aristarchus

Apennine Mountains

Lunar Triangle

Copernicus

Marsh of Sleep

Kepler

Langrenus

Grimaldi

Theophilus

Ptolemaeus

Gassendi

Vendelinus

Petavius

Furnerius

Tycho

Schickard

Lunar Activity #4

Use binoculars to see the brightest craters and mountains. This activity is best done over several nights, observing targets located near the terminator.

Clavius

Glossary

Archaeoastronomy: The study of how ancient cultures used the sky.

Asterism: A recognizable pattern of stars that is not an official constellation.

Astrology: An ancient belief system based on the positions of the planets and the Sun (no relation to science).

Astronomical Seasons: Assigning seasons where spring and autumn start on the **equinoxes** and summer and winter start on the **solstices**.

Astronomy: A science based on precise observation of things in space.

Astrophotography: Using a camera to photograph objects in space.

Barycenter: A point around which two objects orbit.

Black Hole: What remains of some large supergiant stars after a supernova.

Celestial Poles: Points in the sky that align with Earth's axis around which the sky appears to rotate.

Circumpolar: A region of the sky near the celestial poles where the stars never dip below the horizon.

Ecliptic: The path the Sun takes across our sky relative to the background stars.

Element: The building blocks of all the "stuff" in the universe. Most of the visible universe is made of an element called hydrogen.

Equinox: When the Sun is directly above the equator and the day and night are the same length (March 21 and September 23).

Exosphere: An extremely thin atmosphere surrounding small objects like Mercury and Earth's Moon.

Halo: A spherical region around our galaxy where globular star clusters are found.

Horizon: Where the land appears to meet the sky.

Kuiper Belt: A disk-shaped region around our solar system containing several dwarf planets like Pluto.

Latitude: A distance, in degrees, from Earth's equator.

Light-Year: A measure of distance equal to how far light travels in one year (9.5 trillion kilometers).

Magnetic Field: Occurs when rotating planets with metal cores act like giant magnets.

Meteorological Seasons: Seasons based on whole months. Summer is June, July, and August, and so on.

Neutron Star: All that remains of a supergiant star after a supernova.

Nuclear Fusion: The process that powers stars, where lighter elements are combined into heavier ones.

Oort Cloud: A spherical region around our solar system where most of the comets originate.

Orbit: The path an object takes in its journey around a planet, star, or moon. For example, planets orbit stars, moons orbit planets, and satellites orbit Earth.

Precession: The slow change in position of Earth's axis over a 23,000-year cycle.

Satellite: A spacecraft, usually uncrewed, that orbits Earth. These are usually designed for communication such as television or for collecting information such as the weather.

Sky Glow: Also known as light pollution, when artificial lights illuminate the sky, blocking our view of the stars.

Solstice: When the Sun reaches its furthest point either north or south (around June 21 and December 21).

Spin Axis: A line running inside Earth, from the North Pole to the South Pole, around which Earth spins.

Supermassive Black Hole: Black holes that are billions of times the mass of our Sun that reside in the center of most large galaxies.

Tidal Locking: When the same side of an object always faces the object it is orbiting.

Variable Stars: Stars that change in brightness and size over a period of days, weeks, months, or years.

Further Reading

The Stars by H. A. Rey. Originally written in 1952 by the author of the Curious George series, this was one of the first books to simplify the stargazing experience for young observers.

Constellation Finder by Dorcas S. Miller. This tiny pocket-size book contains dozens of star maps and displays the constellations as interpreted in many cultures.

Star Tales by Ian Ridpath. This classic reference guide to the constellations chronicles, in great detail, the myths behind each constellation.

NightWatch by Terence Dickinson. This is one of the most treasured stargazing manuals of all time. Contains very detailed star maps and comprehensive descriptions of all types of celestial objects.

21st Century Atlas of the Moon by Charles A. Wood and Maurice J. S. Collins. This book gives a close look at Earth's nearest neighbor with fantastic imagery from lunar orbiting spacecraft. Designed to help you navigate the Moon from your own backyard.

https://figuresinthesky.visualcinnamon.com. This website explores how the myths of many cultures are represented in the stars.

Image Credits

Primary telescope view images taken by the author. Certain lunar and planetary images were created using data from Stellarium or NASA's visualization studio.

Constellation illustrations created by Ford Rasmussen over Stellarium star fields.

All other image credits provided below:

Adobe Stock: pages 4–5, 6–7 (background and bottom right), 8–9 (background and top center), 12, 14 (background), 16–17, 18 (silhouette), 19 (silhouette), 22–23, 68–69 (all), 70–71, 73, 75 (background), 76–77 (background), 82 (right), 96 (bottom left)

CALTECH/NASA: page 11 (Black Hole)

Dave Chapman/Burke-Gaffney Observatory: page 90 (top right)

ESA/ATG MediaLab: page 72 (bottom left)

ESA/NASA/JPL/University of Arizona: page 87 (bottom right)

ESA/Rosetta/NAVCAM: page 72 (bottom right)

Ford Rasmussen: page 14 (center right)

John A. Read: page 6 (bottom left), 8 (bottom), 9 (Top right, top left, bottom right, bottom left), 11 (top center and Planetary Nebula), 14 (right), 15 (top right, center right), 19 (middle left), 57 (bottom right), 72 (top right), 74 (background), 75 (left), 76–77 (orbits), 94 (bottom right), 96 (all right), 104 (left, center, right bottom)

NASA: page 74 (left, right), 78 (Mercury), 79 (top left), 80 (blimp), 82 (left), 83 (bottom), 84 (all), 86 (left), 88 (background, center, bottom center left), 92–93 (background)

NASA/Applied Physics Laboratory: page 91 (top right)

NASA/ESA/Allison Loll/Jeff Hester/Davide De Martin: page 11 (Supernova)

NASA/ESA/D. PLAYER/STSCI: page 11 (Neutron Star)

NASA/ESA/Hubble Heritage (STScI/AURA)/ESA/Hubble Collaboration: page 51 (bottom)

NASA/GSFC/Arizona State University: page 99

NASA/GSFC/SDO: page 10 (lower left), 11 (Giant Star and white dwarf)

NASA/Johns Hopkins University Applied Physics Laboratory/Southwest Research Institute: page 90 (left, bottom right), 91 (bottom left, bottom right),

NASA/JPL/Caltech: page 88 (bottom right)

NASA/JPL/Caltech/Space Science Institute: page 87 (bottom left)

NASA/JPL/CalTech/University of Arizona: page 83 (top left, top center)

NASA/JPL/DLR: page 85 (bottom right)

NASA/JPL/University of Arizona: page 85 (bottom left)

NASA/JPL/USGS: page 13 (bottom right)

NASA/JPL/Voyager-ISS/Justin Cowart: page 89 (background)

NASA/JPL: page 85 (center right), 86 (right), 87 (center), 88 (bottom left, bottom center, bottom center right)

NASA/PlanetUser; page 89 (bottom left)

NOAA: page 85 (center left)

Reimund Bertrams: page 81 (bottom)

Scott Ward: page 3, 11 (Regular Star, Red Giant, and Super Red Giant), 18–19 (Sun),

Stellarium: page 2, 13 (bottom left, bottom left center, bottom right center), 18–19 (background and Earths), 20, 21, 24, 25, 32, 33, 40, 46, 47, 56, 57 (background), 61 (bottom right), 64, 78–79 (background), 85 (top right), 87 (top right), 89 (top right), 92 (center), 94–95 (background), 104 (background)

Tiffany Fields: page 36 (center right)

www.lightpollutionmap.info: page 15 (bottom right)

How to Use Binoculars
Binocular Setup

Step 1: Look through the binoculars at a faraway target, and adjust the binoculars around the central hinge so that an image is centered in each eye.

Step 2: Close the eye with the diopter, and adjust the focus wheel so that the open eye image is in focus.

Step 3: Switch which eye is closed. Adjust the diopter until that eye is in focus. Open both eyes. When you need to refocus, only use the focus wheel.

How to Use a Telescope
Basic Telescope Setup[1]

Step 1: Set the telescope outside on solid ground with a clear view of the sky.

Step 2: Place a low power (high focal length) eyepiece in the telescope. Do not attach any barlows.

Step 3: Align the finder to the telescope using a distant object such as a lamppost or chimney. The telescope and finder must be pointed at exactly the same spot.

Step 4: Focus the telescope by pointing it at a bright star and turning the focus knob until the star is as small as possible.

[1]There are many different types of telescopes, but these tips will help with all designs. You can find videos on your specific type of telescope at LearnToStargaze.com.

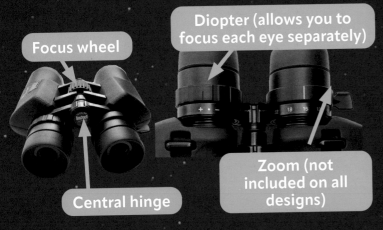

Focus wheel

Diopter (allows you to focus each eye separately)

Central hinge

Zoom (not included on all designs)

Finder alignment screws

Finder

Eyepiece

90° Diagonal

Focus Knob

Mount with up-down and left-right controls

Finding Targets in the Sky

Step 1: Find your target without the binoculars. If you can't see it with the unaided eye, use a map to determine exactly where the target is.

Step 2: With your eyes fixed on your target, slowly move the binoculars up to your face.